Asthma

By Sharon Gordon

Consultants
Nanci R. Vargus, Ed.D.
Assistant Professor
Literacy Education
University of Indianapolis
Indianapolis, Indiana

Jayne L. Waddell, R.N., M.A., L.P.C.
School Nurse/Health Educator/Lic. Professional Counselor

Children's Press®
A Division of Scholastic Inc.
New York   Toronto   London   Auckland   Sydney
Mexico City   New Delhi   Hong Kong
Danbury, Connecticut

Designer: Herman Adler Design
Photo Researcher: Caroline Anderson
The photo on the cover shows a boy using an inhaler.

Library of Congress Cataloging-in-Publication Data

Gordon, Sharon.
  Asthma / by Sharon Gordon.
      p. cm. — (Rookie read-about health)
Summary: Explains what asthma is, what causes asthma attacks, and some
common treatments.
  ISBN 0-516-22582-0 (lib. bdg.)   0-516-27395-7 (pbk.)
  1. Asthma in children—Juvenile literature. [1. Asthma. 2. Diseases.]
I. Title. II. Series.
  RJ436.A8 G66 2003
  618.92'238—dc21   2002015130

JE
GOR
c. 1

$4/14.25$

CHILDREN'S PRESS, AND ROOKIE READ-ABOUT®,
and associated logos are trademarks and or registered trademarks
of Grolier Publishing Co., Inc. SCHOLASTIC and associated logos
are trademarks and or registered trademarks of Scholastic Inc.

1 2 3 4 5 6 7 8 9 10 R 12 11 10 09 08 07 06 05 04 03

Do you know someone with asthma (AS-ma)?

4

Maybe it is a friend.
Maybe it is you!

Many people have asthma,
especially children.

People with asthma sometimes have trouble breathing.

This is called having an *asthma attack*.

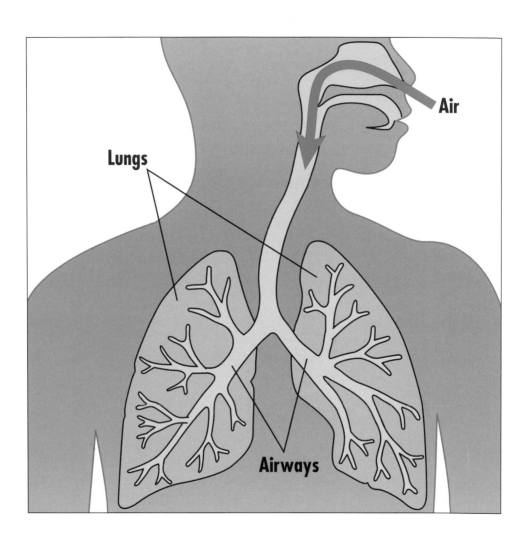

Air

Lungs

Airways

When you breathe, air goes into your lungs.

It travels through tiny tubes called airways.

If you are having an asthma attack, your airways tighten. It is hard for air to get into your lungs.

Your chest feels heavy. You want to take a deep breath, but you cannot.

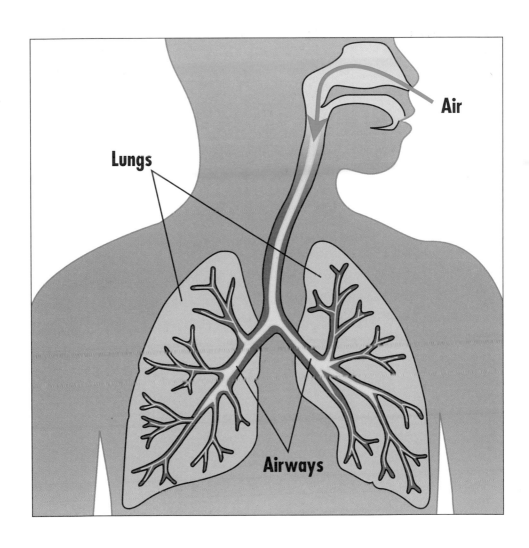

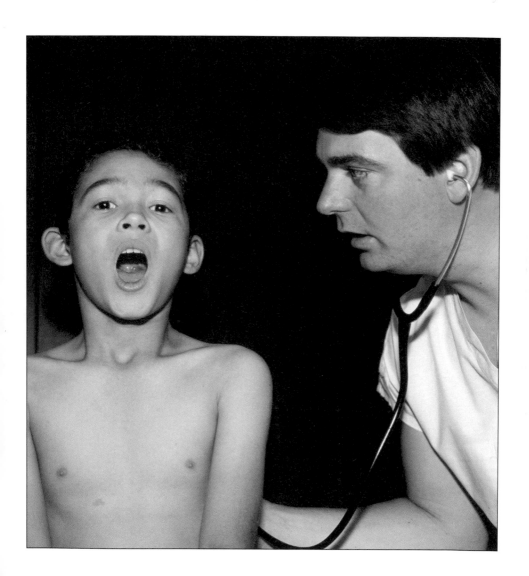

You start to wheeze,
or make strange sounds.
You cough to try to clear
your lungs.

People with asthma need
help from a doctor.

They may have to breathe in medicine through an inhaler (in-HAIL-er).

Once in a while, they might even have to go to the hospital.

No one knows for sure
what causes asthma.
But we do know what
starts an asthma attack.

People with asthma often
have *allergies* (AL-er-jees).

If they breathe in, touch,
or eat certain things, they
may get sick.

An allergy can start an
asthma attack.

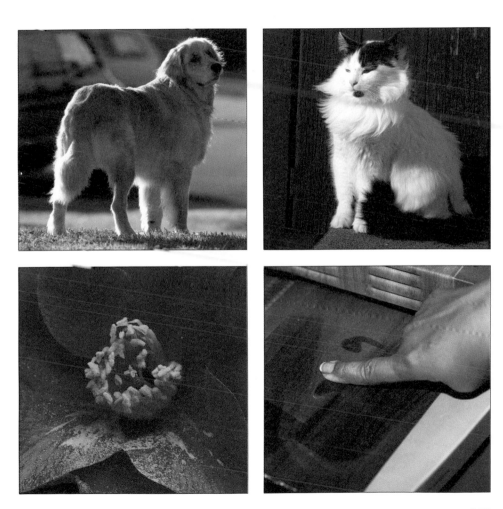

People with asthma
must be careful at other
times, too.

A bad cold or too much
exercise can start an attack.

People with asthma usually have it all their lives.

Some people have fewer attacks as they get older.

They might even stop having attacks.

Having asthma changes your life, but you can learn to live with asthma.

Stay away from things
that start an attack.

Sometimes that might
be hard!

If you are having an asthma attack, try to stay calm.

Take your medicine. It will work quickly.

Soon the attack will be over.

Now you can go back
to having fun!

Words You Know

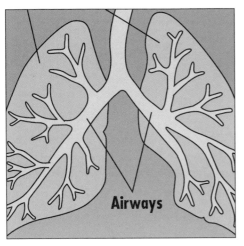

airways

asthma attack

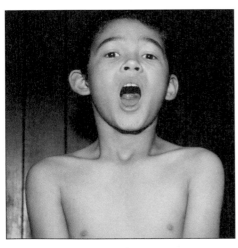

breathing

cough

hospital

inhaler

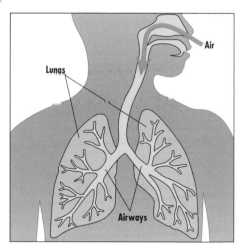

lungs

31

Index

About the Author

Sharon Gordon is a writer living in Midland Park, New Jersey. She and her husband have three school-aged children and a spoiled pooch. Together they enjoy visiting the Outer Banks of North Carolina as often as possible.

Photo Credits

Photographs © 2003: Corbis Images: 26 (Angela Hampton/Ecoscene), 12, 30 bottom left (Brian A. Vikander), 18, 30 bottom right (Jennie Woodcock/ Reflections Photolibrary); Dembinsky Photo Assoc.: 4, 21 (Dan Dempster), 22 (Mark E. Gibson), 17 top right (Gijsbert van Frankenhuyzen); Photo Researchers, NY: 17 top left (Tim Davis), 15, 31 top left (David M. Grossman), 17 bottom left (Gail Jankus); PhotoEdit: 29 (Myrleen Ferguson Cate), cover, 7, 14, 30 top right, 31 top right (David Young-Wolff); Rigoberto Quinteros: 17 bottom right; The Image Works: 3 (Michael J. Doolittle), 25 (Willie Hill, Jr.).